Muse

Samuel Gluck

Muse
Samuel Gluck

Email: hello@orenaugmountainpublishing.com
Website: www.orenaugmountainpublishing.com

ISBN: 979-8-9925369-2-8

Printed in the United States of America

These musings have accumulated over 55 years
in many different times and places and
would not be possible without the love and support of my family
Alanna, Dana, and Linda

And especially for the encouragement
and the gift of the love of Muriel

Muse

An instance or period of deep thought or dreamy abstraction
A source of inspiration...focused daydreaming as in remembrance
A person or imaginary being or force that gives someone ideas
and helps them to paint write or make music
A poet

Author's Note

In these poems you might notice an absence of punctuation, except in cases where there is dialogue, and where it is necessary to be clear about the words being spoken in conversation rather than narration.

The omission of punctuation is meant to create or enhance ambiguity, emotion, urgency, visual impact and poetic license in order to allow the reader to interpret the poem through their eyes.

Table of Contents

Forever Grateful

Forever grateful am I for
The many gifts I have been given
For all the songs I have played
And for the poems I have written

Forever blessed am I
To look up at the sky
To feel the ground beneath my feet
To see the love in your eye

How wondrous it is
To feel the sun on my face
To see the clouds fly by
To see the stars in the dark of space

Forever thankful am I
To my mother and my father
It could have been a lot easier
But could have been a lot harder

How fortunate am I
To meditate on my breath
To enjoy this day of life
And delay my date with death

How happy am I
To enjoy my given time
To reflect on the divine
And share these words of rhyme

Gift of Life

In the twilight of the evening
Through the black and dark of night
Comes a glimmer then a sparkle
Came the dawn of new morning light

The sun is rising, the darkness fading
Birds are flying and singing bright
Angels are landing bringing greetings
Everything will be alright

What a present what a blessing
To greet each new day and the gift of life
Giving thanks for each new morning
Throughout the day and every night

Amino Acids

Amino acids in an ancient ocean
A long time ago
Joining uniting bonding
Forming complex chains
Dividing into cells–male/female
Growing developing into beings
Of movement instinct intelligence
The male swimming in darkness
A journey–the odds of surviving
So small–propelled by nature and destiny
To change into one new soul

Swimming now in clear waters
Separate and equal under sun and moon
Aquamarine shining are your eyes
Light surrounded by flesh
Immersed now in waters fresh
Grown cells–female/male–
Young old timeless
Light in your smile

A Poem

A poem
a moment frozen
in time
made crystalline
held up to shine
through the rays of the sun
to see its refraction
into colored beams of light
each with an interpretation or insight
to see what it is
that we wish it to be
just like you, just like me.

A poem
an instant chosen
not to fade away
into the distant memory
but to always stay
as an ever present reality
an experience to be relived
in a moment's notice
to bring one nearest
to what is dearest
in the soul in the heart
not even death can tear it apart.

A poem
a time defined
into immortality
much more than a dream
that passes through the night
to be forgotten
but a glimpse of reality
caught in a split second of clarity
and seen with eyes wide open
on the screen of eternity
just like you, just like me.

Blinded by the Sun

All I really want to do
      Is get away from you
            Ain't feeling blue
All I really gotta say
      I'm getting on my way
            So have a nice day

I just wanted to be real
      To tell you how I feel
            How come you can't deal
I was moving way too fast
      Was burning all my gas
            Now it's all in the past

I really thought you were the one
      I was blinded by the sun
            I ain't getting fooled again
                  That's right babe
                      I ain't getting fooled again

You have that kind of look
      I know you like a book
            It pulls me like a hook
We were having so much fun
      I was blinded by the sun
            So sad it's all done

Hope I see another ray
      Come another day
            Love will come my way

I really thought you were the one
      I was blinded by the sun
            I ain't getting fooled again
                 That's right babe
                     I ain't getting fooled again

Hey girl go to school
      I ain't your fool
            What you think
                 Your shit don't stink

Catch Me if You Can

What am I, and who are you
And what are you holding in your hand
Are your eyes moving your mind spinning
your heart feeling your spirit soaring
What is it exactly you are imagining

Am I a thought a mood
Insight or spark of spirit channeled by hand
Points of ink a string of letters
Arranged according to your random plan
Scattered lines on a page
Creating images or feelings to gauge
Be they silly petty profound or sage

I float through space time
The here and the now
The before and the after and beyond the beyond
I am in galaxies in black holes and all spaces in between
In quarks mesons and ions
in every soul I can be seen
In infinity and eternity I am unbound

If you try or believe
You might catch me if you can
Arrange me in any order
And come to understand
That I come not from you but in and through
I am that I am
You may catch me if you can

City Blues

City blues got a hold on you
You want to live the life
but you don't have a clue

Uptown blues got you strung real tight
You want to live the life
But you can't sleep at night

You want to live the life but you haven't got a plan
What you need is a real good man
City blues got a hold on you
And you just don't know what to do

East side blues hit you in the gut
You want to live the life but you're in a rut
Downtown blues got you really down
You want to live the life all over town

You want to live the life and you haven't got a plan
What you need is a real good man
City blues got a hold on you
And you just don't know what to do

You're looking for a man with a whole lotta money
What you really need is a real sweet honey
Big city blues got you in a rut
Hot city mama I'm gonna look you up

You want to live the life and you haven't got a plan
Look here baby I'm your man
City blues got a hold on you
There's just nothing to do

Dark of Night

My love calls to me in the dark of night
My love comes to me like a flower to light
She kisses me so tenderly
We make love so completely
My love comes to me in the dark of night

My love comes to me she brings me wine
We're drawn together two of a kind
We kiss and kiss we just can't miss
We touch so much we're in our bliss
My love talks to me in the dark of night

My love speaks to me in the dark of night
My love touches me and holds me tight
We move we sit then kiss some more
Into each other's soul we pour
My love makes love with me in the dark of night

Force Magnetic

Is that what you felt when my pixels formed on your screen
And your finger went click
A force magnetic
Is that what you recognized when we met face to face
And you smiled
A force electric
Is that what you wanted when I sat next to you
The first time
A force kinetic
Is that what you longed for when you came to my place
And never left
A force volcanic
Is that what you feel in our embrace
every day and every night
In the dark or by the dawning light
Skin on skin mouth on mouth
Limbs entwined minds that shine
Face to face eye to eye
Heart to heart soul to soul
In our warmth and out from the cold
Do you ever wonder why
The force majestic

Destination

I was walking down the road one day
and nothing seemed the same
it seemed I had lost my way
I couldn't even remember my name
Night was falling and there I was stranded in the dark
so I decided to sit myself down on a nearby rock

Suddenly a stranger appeared
and I was taken aback
I didn't know where I was
or how to get back on track
I asked the stranger where I was
and he said to have no fear
"Son" he said "I don't know where YOU are
but I know that I am here"

So I said "I don't know what to do
or which way I should go
maybe you can set me straight
And point me to the right road"

"You could go right or to the left
so I don't know where you're heading
best to break right on through
and face whatever it is you are dreading
there's a door to a tunnel straight ahead
that will take you in your direction
It may be dark or may be bright
but might clear up your perception"

"Well how will I know where I'm going
if I don't have a map
Cause I lost my phone and I can't see
and I don't have that app"

The stranger smiled and said "Listen very carefully
to these words that will set you free
you may find loss
or you may find gain
you might have joy
or you may feel pain
but for this I'm sure
if you don't open that door
You will never find what it is
that you are looking for"

"Thank you kind sir
for all your information
Now I know what to do
and how to arrive at my destination"
And one more thing I asked
to the kind stranger
"What is your name and thank you
for keeping me out of danger"

The stranger looked me in the eye
and said these words to me
"You know who I am
I am you and you are me
and our name is Sam"

Force of Nature

You're a hurricane you're a tropical storm
Whoever you are you're not the norm
You're a force of nature and a sight to behold
But sorry baby this affair is getting old

I'm up north and you're down south
I love ya baby and I love your mouth
But you're always telling me what to do
Well if you're so smart what ya gonna do about you

You're a tornado you're a cyclone
You're a thousand miles from my home
You're a force of nature and a sight to behold
But sorry baby this affair has gotten old

Forest Maiden

Forest maiden of the summer wood
Oh if I only could
Stay for another hour another day
So that we could find all there is to say
And see and feel
Breathe deeply and real

The look on your face so soft and young
Innocent and fair
With your green eyes and your blonde hair
More than worthy of all the love poetry ever written
A meager mortal attempt at a heart expression

My dear forest maiden
I can only be grateful to know you
Thankful to hold you
Special to kiss you
And blessed sweet lady to love you

Go with the Flow

Like a tiger in the night
I just want a little bite
Hungry lion on the roam
I wanna bring you home

When you get that urge
That you wanna merge
Feel that sudden surge
Just take it slow
You gonna reap what you sow
Just want ya to know to go with the flow

Like a bitch in heat
You're such a tasty treat
Horny buck on a doe
Ya just gotta know
Sleek panther on the hunt
Lookin for a piece of rump
Shark swimming in the deep
Lookin for a piece of meat

When you get that urge
That you wanna merge
Feel that sudden surge
Just take it slow
You gonna reap what you sow
Just want ya to know to go with the flow

Lucky leopard on a kill
You're such a thrill
So *au naturel*
Well well well

Wild wolf on the prowl
I'm gonna make ya howl
Said the fox to the sheep
I just wanna eat

When you get that urge
That you wanna merge
Feel that sudden surge
Just take it slow
You gonna reap what you sow
Just want ya to know to go with the flow

You're pumping through my veins
Like a runaway train
We're gettin ready to explode
So just go with the flow

Golden Lions

In the inky blue of a cloudy night
Through soft luminous moonlight
Two golden lions in flight
Racing to hold each other tight

Onto the field they race
Panting at a passionate pace
She turns he sees her face
Such is the heat of the race

Later at rest under a tree
In darkness their eyes clearly see
Each into the other's so easily
That I love you and you know me

Frozen Moments

Shimmering glistening crystallizing
      Against sky so blue air so dry
            Clouds so high
                 My oh my
Vapors emit like erupting volcanoes
      Of flowing molten fire
            Vulcanized to inspire
The cold and the heat
      The bitter and the sweet
            The earth and the sky
                 The beauty of you and I

Goddamn Blues

I'm sitting here all alone
just wondering what to do
Hanging out by the phone
but there ain't nothing new
Thinking about the days gone by
and all the fun we had
It makes me want to cry
makes me feel so sad

Once I was a young man
Now I am so old
I used to be so hot
But now I feel so cold
Once I was a young man
And I had a lot of fun
But now I'm just an old man
And I'm having none

I think I'll go to the bar
And get myself a drink
Ain't gonna go too far
Cause I need some time to think
I think I'll find a lover
I'll find somebody new
We'll get under the covers
And fuck these goddamn blues

Once I was a young man
I used to play the game
Now I'm an old man
And I feel so lame

Once I was a young man
I used to feel so strong
Now I'm an old man
And everything feels so wrong

Oh dear Lord what can I say
Is it time to pray
Hey God what's the deal
Is reality real
I pray to Jesus and I hail to Mary
But this whole world is driving me crazy
Would'a, should'a, wished I coulda
Can you free me Buddha

I'll get on the net
And find myself a date
You never know what you'll get
So I leave it up to fate
I'm looking for a woman
I'll find somebody new
Just tired of being alone
Fuck these goddamn blues

Once I was a young man
Now I am so old
I used to be so hot
Now I feel so cold
Once I was a young man
I used to be in the game
Now I'm just an old man
Can't even remember my name

Hey mister minister
Why is the world so sinister
Hey church father
Can it get any harder
Hey mister imam
Go and eat a bomb
Hey mister rabbi
All I want to know is why

Great Mother

So luscious and succulent
      Your fruits of spring
Soft firm flesh oozes in my mouth
      Juices through my lips
           On my tongue
                Down my throat
Sweet ecstasy fills me with energy
      Of water earth and air
           Rushing through my arteries and veins
              Like your life-giving rains
      Flowing through brooks and streams
           Turning the ground vibrantly green
              Filling me with all that is under the sun
             You in me, me in you
            Become one

Help Me, Dear Jesus

I got fired from my job
My boss is an ass
What am I gonna say to my wife
I work hard all my life
And I can't get ahead
Sometimes I think I'd be better off dead

Don't talk to my kids
They think I'm lame
Why is life filled with such shame
I can't catch a break
I've been down on my luck
Why do I feel like such a dumb schmuck

It's so hard to try, and I don't want to fail
Help me dear Jesus and lend me a nail

Didn't want to be bald
But I lost all my hair
Why is life so unfair
I just want to be cool
But I'm big and fat
So I'll just pull down my truck drivin' hat

It's so hard to try, and I don't want to fail
Help me dear Jesus and lend me a nail

I'm a two-time loser
But now is my chance
I'm beginning to see the light
There's a girl over there
She looks like a boozer
I think this time I'll be getting it right
It's so hard to try and I don't want to fail
Help me dear Jesus and lend me a nail

It's so hard to try and I'm out on bail
Help me dear Jesus I just got out of jail

I Am

I am a human being
Created in the image of God
I am a Man
Of this there is no doubt
Determined by countless generations which preceded me
And by chromosomes named X and Y
I am a Man
I know this to be the truth by looking in the mirror
And pleased with who is looking back at me
I greet each day grateful to be alive and thankful that
I am a Man
I recognize the female within me as I am a
Reflection of my mother who bore me
By my sisters who adored me
And by the women who have loved me because
I am a Man
I am a Son
I honor my father and my mother who gave me
The gift of life and raised me to know that
I am a Man
I am a Soul
Which is eternal surrounded and embodied in flesh
Which is constantly changing as does all creation
I am a Man
I know the light in my eyes and the light in the sun is the same light
The space within me and the space without
Is the space in which I am
Because I know that
I am a Man

I am an energy field

I have the power to attract and repel and will manifest into my reality

That which I desire because

I am a Man

I had a beginning which is called birth

And I will have an end which is known as death

Everything in between is the gift of life

I know this to be the ultimate truth and I have no fear

I am a man

I See My Love

I see my love
In the stillness of a summer day
Hot sun crackling dry
Spiritually high ready to fly

I see my love
On the canyon rim
Strong firm and free
Embracing the journey and what it will be

I see my love
Resting on a rattlesnake's rock
Sun-drenched energized
Growing steady and ready to thrive

I see my love
Running through the field
Flying through time and space
With that glowing look on your face

I see my love
On the mountain top
Wind blowing through your hair
Climbing high without a care

I see my love
Silhouetted against the sky
With that lovely prophetic look
Writing this poem in this book

In the Forest

In the forest in the dark of night
      The lovers lay by candlelight
Arm in arm not an inch apart
      Speaking softly about matters of the heart
As if the mind could fathom
      That which cannot be understood
That which countless lovers have shared
      Or those without desperately wish they could
The great eternal mystery
      The elusive electricity the ultimate victory
         The union of Shiva with Shakti
The sweetest fruits of life the finest wine
      Love comes not from the earth
         It is the light of the Divine

Is It or It Is

Is it possible to be in two places at the same time
To exist here and now in the physical
      and simultaneously in the metaphysical

Science and or logic would say no
Yet how is it that I am present
      and absent at the same time

To have my feet on the ground
And my head in the clouds
        or up my ass

Like the lotus flower with its roots in the muck
And its lustrous petals open to the sun
        Floating as if suspended
Existing in earth water air and light
      At the same time
        In the same place

Is this phantasmagoria or euphoria
Is this fantasy or reality
      It is it

Island Lady

My ship is entering your harbor island lady
my anchor is plunging heavily headlong
into the soft sandy bottoms of your bay
and I am coming to stay awhile
on your tropical isle
of setting suns and orange skies
moonstruck nights and star shine eyes
of blue violet and purple moons
hanging over lazy lagoons
and your slender palms pulsating in the evening breeze
rustling through the leaves and through your hair
like the breath of a shadow

You are as lovely in the darkness
as you are brilliant in the light
island lady make love with me tonight
live totally in this moment that will last us for a life
make our time tonight timelessly infinite
and let me live forever in your mind and heart
just as I live in every part
of your luscious island home
Just as you've made your way deeply into my soul

January Skies

Azure blue fills late January skies
The color of your eyes
Late afternoon sun streaks golden rays
Into the strands of your hair
Light fills your smiling face
As we meet touch and again embrace

Surprisingly still standing vertically
Balancing on three feet
Like a strange creature or unknown beast
Or like a strong vine wrapped tightly around a tree
While beckons the horizontal plane
Like winter's frozen earth thawing in the spring rain

Jewels of Life

Flowing moments of closeness kindness
Touching holding wearing
On my neck arms and fingers
Priceless jewels strung together on the
Line of time
Like a necklace of my mind

Precious instances
Of smiling laughter in colors
Like rubies emeralds pearls and aquamarines
Shaped like raindrops wrapped around your wrist
Like a bracelet of the heart

Glistening golden is the early morning light
The sun reflecting the turning autumnal leaves
Love beams like diamonds from your eyes
Enveloping like a ring of the soul
The jewels of life

Lion Wolf

Am I the wolf who roams the night
Am I the lion soaking in the sun
I am love
I make two into one

You are the warmth
You are the hearth
In your embrace
I am home

What was never gained
Cannot be lost
Love is priceless
There is no cost
Life is change
Change is growth
Whatever happens to us both
Love is

Lioness

He tells her he thanks God every morning
For another day of life and the gift he was sent

She asks where he came from
And how his life has been spent

The same place as you he replies
As he points to her heart and looks into her eyes

When she is gone he returns into aloneness
And realizes how precious is their togetherness

The lion and the wolf await the return
Of the lovely sweet golden-haired lioness

Land of Adornment

Like a dream from the land of adornment
A Tibetan scene
Of pristine snow white or
summer vivid green
A glimpse of a place both far and near
Hidden by fog or shining so clear
A place safe calm and serene
An outward reflection of the inner life stream

Like a photographic negative in black and white
Striving to overcome the dualities of pain in life to unite
Looking and questioning all without answers
While ever present sits the enlightened master

Introspection meditation self-examination
Please tell me dear master
The answer to this question
Oh Great Lord of Light
Grant me the perfection of your insight
Is there an answer to the human plight

"Attachment and desire cause all pain and suffering .
So just give and love and please stop asking"

The Material

If you are looking for the material you may well succeed
But probably won't realize what it is that you truly need
The years move on and our looks do fade
The body changes and heads into retrograde
Truth is the realm of the heart and the soul
What is everlasting from time immemorial
For love my dear is the greatest goal
The bringing of two souls into one new whole

Man About Town

I love the country I like to sing
I dig most anything
I like the city I'm in the know
We can take it slow
I'll do anything that I can
If you'll let me be your man
I'm a man about town I get around
How about you

I met a babe the other night
She was hot out of sight
She asked me what I do
I said baby how about you
I go to a disco and start to dance
I'll fly you to Paris France
I'll do anything you want me to
So I can make love to you

I'll do anything that I can
If you'll let me be your man
I'm a man about town
I get around
How about you

One day I'll be old and gray
It will be a real fine day
Till then I'll just fool around
Until they put me in the ground
I pray to God up above
If you will be my love
I'll do anything you want me to
So I can make love with you

I'll do anything that I can
If you'll let me be your man
I'm a man about town
I get around
How about you

OMG

What is to become of me
I'm not quite the man I used to be

All my energies have been spent
Now feeling drained weak frail and bent
Once there burnt so hot a fire
To satisfy each and every desire

OMG what is to become of me
I'm not quite the man I used to be

My get up and go
Has got up and went
Barely have the strength
To follow up the scent

Once I was a rooster
Playing amongst the chicks
Would preen and strut my stuff
I knew all of the tricks

Stayed up all night to crow at dawn
Greeted each new day at the rising sun
Now I crawl to sleep at evening's fall
When the day is done and my world's gone small

OMG what is to become of me
I'm not quite the man I used to be

Once I was a lion
Would reign over my pride
All would be rivals
Would run away and hide

Once I was the lead wolf
The alpha of my pack
Now I am all alone
And looking over my back

Once I was an eagle
Soaring in the sky
Can barely spread my wings now
To fly back on high

OMG what is to become of me
I'm not quite the man I used to be

To all the friends and loves I have known
Thanks for all the love you've shown
You didn't stick around all that long
So for all of you I sing this song

OMG what is to become of me
I'm not quite the man I used to be

Match

If you're feeling lonely log onto Match.com
You may get lucky or you could hit a bomb
Just a click and find yourself a date
You may get lucky and find your new soulmate

He may be short she could be tall
Don't really matter much at all
She could be poor he could be rich
Could be a bore could be a bitch

Anything can happen when you get on to Match.com
Just be cool and be real calm
Just a click and find yourself a date
You may get lucky and find your new soulmate

I saw your pic up on my screen
Maybe baby you will be my queen
You like to go all around the world
Can I take you for a whirl

Anything can happen when you get onto Match.com
You could be a dad or you could be a mom
Don't really know who you are
But for 20 bucks a month you can be a star

Do you yoga so glad to know ya
I can say Namaste
You like to dance you like to dine
Can I meet ya for a glass of wine

Anything can happen when you get onto Match.com
You could be lucky, or you could hit a bomb
Just a click, don't hesitate
You may get lucky and find your new soulmate

Anybody see a soulmate
I know you're around here somewhere
Oh well
I think I'll find another date

Matters of the Heart

Do you miss me in our absence
Do you miss yourself as part of us
Wherever I am there you are
The whole is so much greater
Than the sum of the parts
That's how it is with matters of the heart

If I focus on the part that you are
I will miss you I will long for you
Though hard to admit
I know it to be true
Better that I see the whole that we are
That's how it is with matters of the heart

Mountain Queen

My summer maiden my mountain queen
I can't believe what I have seen
While walking on my hilltop trail
I came upon a golden cat she lifted her tail
Our eyes met our gaze locked
I was so aroused I was fully cocked
She asked me to lie with her in the soft grass
Then she gave me her beautiful ass
I felt so big I thought I would explode
But I was able to save my load
We rocked and reeled in the summer heat
We made exquisite love from head to feet
Many hours passed–four five six
I can't get enough may I have another lick
I wish to be with her on our mountain retreat
Shaded from the August heat
If we get too hot I know a private pool
We'll swim and play get wet and cool
Then come close again
Just say when just say when
Reminds me when the grass was gold
When I was new with my love of old
We laid on a stone then with a view
If way back then we only knew
That a few seasons later in the middle of summer
I'd come for you I am your lover

First Day of Spring

Waves of life force moving through space
Tides of breath fill the air
The ebb and the flow fill my pores
Filter through my cells
Merge into my core
Light fills the sky
Entering through my eyes into my being
Grass greening and flowers breaking ground
Channels of energy streaming
Their currents growing strong
Day equals night
Balance
First day of Spring 2025
I am alive

Thoughts

Emanating from the Cosmic Mind
of Beingness, Consciousness
into particles and waves
traveling at the speed of light
becoming and ending
In Matter and Antimatter.
Stars expanding and imploding
into black holes
Expanse and density
Fate and destiny
Atoms and galaxies
Finite and infinite
Being and non being
Thoughts of the mind

Ms. Fine

Forty-eight hours around the sun
Impossible to comprehend what has just begun
From a like and a meet a look and hello
Can tell the heart the soul all there is to know
A magnetization of unfathomable attraction
Like undercurrents moving deep under the ocean
Or seismic manifestations creating tectonic motion
Your look and smile your lips so sublime
Your essence your scent so sweet and divine
My dear Ms Fine will you be my valentine

Muse

Awaiting you my muse
for our final chapter
Siren beauty of spirit
Light love and laughter
Heartfelt soul filled with unbounded kindness
My vixen my fox
Dearest lioness goddess

My Movie (The Story of Me)

Many are the stories in the theatre of my mind
Whether real or imaginary they compel me to find
If it is real or only just a dream
Is it permanent or only a passing scene

Moving images fly by like clouds in the sky
Sometimes so obscured that I cannot discern
Sometimes so dazzlingly bright at other times so dark
Pictures projected onto the screen of my mind

Is it a comedy or a tragedy
A documentary or merely a fantasy
It might be a romance or a horror story
Most likely a drama depending on the karma

You might be the star or just passing through
Could last a lifetime or somebody new
So many characters always coming and going
All the while the signs of aging are showing

How this movie ends I don't really know
It's been going on for quite a while one hell of a show
This much I can say after all this time
I am glad I stuck around because this movie is mine

Ode to a Cup

Oh wouldst that I were able
to have a seat at thy table
To drink contently from thy cup
with breakfast lunch and sup
to taste thy wine so fine
and quench this thirst of mine

Oh wouldst that I were able
to share a seat at thy table
and taste thy fruits so sweet
Oh would thee I entreat
I'd ravage thy cupboards bare
such delicacies beyond compare
and gladly return for more
for thy endless bounty would restore

Oh wouldst if I were able
to lay my plate upon thy table
Will this hunger not abate
for a morsel a piece a taste
Will my cup go unfilled
Say you will...say you will
Oh wouldst that I were able
to fill my cup upon thy table

Ode to a Greek Goddess

Like Aphrodite Athena and Artemis
I have seen a golden Greek goddess
Statuesque graceful strong and firm
I look into her eyes and see stars shine
I look to the moon and see spirit fly
I look to the ground and see her run
Fleet swift strong
It is her nature an intuition
Like an unseen river deep underground
A powerful current the sound
I can feel her come
Roaring to merge with the ocean

Ode to Spring (Or a Romantic Spring Fever)

Ode to thee fair maiden of spring
Praises of love to thee I do sing
Your trees now in blossom your fields turning green
Honored and awed am I by your beauty just seen

Sweet lily fair lilac dearest flower of purple
You make my soul quiver you make my heart gurgle
Your petals so lovely so exquisite your scent
Such beauty to behold a sensual intoxicant

So soft is thy belly so full is thy breast
My face my head I pray on thee may I rest
May I climb on thy mountains and lay in thy valleys
My rivers my streams join in the blue of thy seas

In the dark of the night my love calleth to me
Neither shadows nor dreams can block the light that I see
Our bodies touch our mouths again meet
So total the comfort our kisses so sweet

United embraced into each other we melt
So familiar it seems so deeply love felt
The greatest gift just given separate lives made whole
You fulfilled my self you restored my soul

Now knowing the truth which was recently guessed
No longer a wonder our minds now at rest
Dearest maiden of spring my cup runneth over
Sweet lily fair lilac wilt thou beest my lover

On the Mountain

High on the mountain
Perched in a tree
Breathlessly waiting
Something to come to me
Along stirs a breeze
Ready to please
And once again I am on the trapeze

I look to the sky
To steady my heart
I look to the mind ready to start
Poised now on a precipice high
I am ready to spring eager to fly
Ready to look at fear in the face
Willing to jump into the unknown space
I know you are with me I feel your grace

One Heart

One heart beating in two separate lives
One cup filling from the river running wide
One shared memory of divine place and time
Still and yet to be

Ancient paths intersected
Stir the fires of buried needs
Newly resurrected

Hovering above an uncertain volcano
Will the boiling molten lava ebb or flow
Will she sing her siren songs for his soul to hear
Will he strum his secret chords to quiet her fear

Piece of Cloth

Torn from the same piece of cloth
Velvet or wool cotton or silk
Jagged and crooked
And cut from the same ilk
Ragged and frayed
Weathered and stained
Never meeting or sharing
Neither pleasure nor pain

Through seasons years decades and a life
Lives filled with happiness loneliness pain and strife
Places near and familiar with similar family ties
Vows and promises taken then broken with lies
Now two pieces joined together as one piece of cloth
Attracted to each other like the flame and the moth

Prince Charming

I am your Prince Charming
And you are my Princess my darling
I will fulfill your every need
In all thoughts actions and deeds
I will be your greatest lover
No need to ever wonder
I will always be truthful and never lie
Swear on my sacred oath until I die
I will be your truest friend
Forever I promise until the end
I will be your hero
Your knight in shining armor
And you will be my fair maiden
No need to look any farther
I am your eternal soulmate
Surely this is our destiny our fate
And you shall be my queen
As I fulfill your every dream
And I will give you my ring
For I am your one true love I am your king

Purdy Gurl

I just can't get you out of my head
Just want to get you in bed
I'm sitting here sad and blue
How am I gonna get through to you

What am I gonna do
To get through to you
What am I gonna say
To get you to come my way

Thinkin 'bout the dates we had
Some were good and some were bad
All I wanted was a kiss goodnight
I didn't want to start a fight

I'm sitting here all alone
I just want you to come back home
I go to call you on your cell-o-phone
But all I get is a busy tone

Where do you want to go
I really gotta know
I'm really gonna try
Without you I'm gonna cry

I think I'll find a new purdy gurl
Someone who won't make me hurl
A real fine woman I can hold real tight
A real hot mama I can kiss all night

Where do you want to go
I really gotta know
I'm really gonna try
Without you I'm gonna die

I just want a purdy gurl
Someone who will make my world
I just want a purdy gurl
I just want a purdy gurl

Garden of Love

In the garden of love
Grows the flower of light
A reflection of the eternal
The clear the great and the bright
Not touching fertile Earth
Still felt so deep
So beautiful to sight
It's scent so sweet
Not nourished by rain
But of itself sustained

In the garden of pure love
Grows the flower of light
Shimmering and effulgent
In the day or at night
Ever present in the mind or to the eye
Rooted to Earth or floating in sky
Revealed to all who open the heart
Who give and share and see with insight

June

It was a day in June
A Gemini full moon
The twins in deep swoon
So in love by strike of noon
Once again standing at the shore
Where they stood a few days before
They came back for more
Like eating an apple to its core
Hearing the ancient sound of the tide
By the river running wide
Sharing feelings that they cannot hide
Though they could have tried
Sharing gifts and exchanging cards
Giving and receiving under bright stars
Though they may journey high and far
In my heart is where you are

Rockin' Bud

I saw you at the show
  You were standing in my row
I saw you dancing in the aisle
  I winked and you smiled

You kept me up all night
  Didn't put up a fight
You're a rock 'n' roll fan
  And I'm the honky-tonk man

I met you at the gig
  You looked at me and I'm getting big
You got those eyes and blonde hair
  You got that look and I don't scare

You kept me up all night
  Didn't put up a fight
You're a rock 'n' roll fan
  I am your ever lovin' man

We saw The Stones we saw The Who
  You got a friend she's wearing blue
We danced with Mick and rocked with Keith
  Didn't miss a step didn't miss a beat

We're gonna rock we're gonna roll
  Go to the bar go for a stroll
In the town that knows no rest
  Don't you know that we're the best

We're throwing dice and pulling spades
      I'm hanging out with all the babes
Feeling good cause I ain't no dud
      Don't you know I'm a rockin' Bud

I'm feeling hot I'm burning up
      I'm going out to all the clubs
Feeling good ain't no stick in the mud
Don't you know that I'm a rockin' Bud

Private Domain

There is a special place my private domain
My home my realm there I reign
Seems like a fairy tale doesn't seem real
Yet I know in my heart what I feel
A beautiful spot by a magical pond
Where an enchanted creature with the wave of a wand
Suddenly appears as if from the beyond
Soft beautiful open to my kisses
She fulfills every desire and all of my wishes
We wave like the grasses and tall trees
Swaying in sweet ecstasy with the summer breeze
Am I dreaming or am I drunk
Must be the sound of the popping champagne cork
At the Ledge named Locke in the town of Yorke

Sand Dunes

Sand dunes dance away with the wind
They change their shape
To its every whim
While turquoise white-capped waves
Whip endlessly against
Black volcanic crags
On the ocean of time

Gushing falls rush tumultuously
Towards wispy wet deep glades
They shake and they sway and
They ebb at their bay
As the dripping rains fall softly
Like tears of joy on a shallow pool
Their ripples reflecting
The light of it all

Scottish Glen

Whilst sitting in a Scottish glen
Came upon me an uncanny yen
Upon my steed I quickly rode
To the nearest pub my spiritual abode
Came to me a lovely lass
With a readied amber filled glass
"What shall your pleasure be
Is it sherried peated smoked or me"
Dear girl I said with due respect
What is it that you truly expect
"Oh kind sir just be real
Is there anything for me you feel"
My feelings for you should certainly come first
But for now I must quench this raging thirst
For though thy beauty is worthy of desire
Within me burns a raging fire
That can only be sated by the master of malt
Sweet lady of mine it is not your fault
For as soon as I drown this yearning of mine
Our pleasures to come shall truly be divine

Seasons of Love

Many seasons passing since our beginning
Summer falling winter springing
Endlessly around turning
Turning into this season of our love

Mornings and evenings
Days spent speaking and learning
Looking and asking
Spring blooming caring sharing turning
Turning into this season of our love

Many are the pictures in the album of my mind
Winter spring summer fall meetings
Mornings and evenings
Summers heating oozing squeezing turning
Turning into this season of our love

Many seasons passing since our beginning

Seed of Love

A seed of love
Carried on the softest breath
From the cosmic wind
Could have blown away
Washed away into oblivion
Leaving not the mark of a speck of dust
Ever to be seen by the naked eye
Human or otherwise
Ever so subtly to take root
Gently and tenderly
Seemingly invisibly
Through cycles and seasons
Passing perhaps for eons
A chance conception an interminable gestation
An act of procreation
A birthing in love making
An ending a beginning a changing
The wheel of karma inevitably turning
Transforming reshaping time and space
For the earthly seedlings

Slainte Mhath

Balvenie or Glen Allachie
Does not matter much to me
Aberlour or Edradour
May I have another pour
GlenDronach or Mortlach
Johnny Red or Johnny Black
Taken neat or with ice
Either way is always so nice
James Grant or Diageo
Oh so right you always know
Highland or Speyside
In your warmth do I abide
By the sea or on the isle
I shall savor you for a while
It matters not on what I think
Just that I can enjoy my drink
Slainte mhath

Sonic Vibrations

Sonic vibrations from the icy deep
Wake my love from her morning sleep
Transfixed and galvanized
Feeling totally awake totally alive
Moving running changing
Are the seasons of our lives
Giving sharing knowing and loving
That living life is not a black and white duality
But part of a far greater reality
And to be high on top of the mountain
With magic and a full heart
Basking in the warmth of the sun
Is to be one with the One

Tess

On a black steed named Tess
Into the wood they sped
And to each did express
In look word and touch
Their need to feed and be fed

Out of the wind out of the cold
A cave they found a home of old
Primitive and deep they did retreat
Into hot fire's glow
Keeping them in heat bonded complete
Like golden mountain lions
Emerging from their den
Into winter's first snow
A sign from the sky
Remembered once again
And again to know

The Mirror

Looking in the mirror
What a revelation
More than just the reflection
Of arms and legs wrapped around each other
By the strength of a calm and steady magnet

An imprint embedded into the body/mind
Impressed like jello poured into a mold
So tightly do our bodies hold
Much more so than the love stains left
To evaporate from your garment

The Son of Cups sings odes
To the sky eyed sun haired goddess
He sits striving for synthesis
Without pain without gain
Immersed in the heat of the radiance

The Ocean

My name is Poseidon hear me roar
I send my waves crashing on your shore
My breath is the wind that brings the tide
When we move feel me rise
We change shapes we ebb and flow
See me now and know
I am Neptune feel my spear
We are safe in our ocean have no fear

The Old White Stallion

See that old white stallion out at pasture
      Gone forever long-lost days of rapture
Fading memories of the glories of the race
      When hooves and hearts were pounding rapidly apace

Out at range now just looking to graze
      Staring off in the distance in a gentle gaze
Roaming lanes and aisles and fields of green
      Past old gray mares never again to be seen

Nary a look nor a smile not much left to see
      Gone forever former days of victories
See that old white stallion out to pasture
      Left only with fading memories of long-lost stature

The Present

He tells her he thanks God every morning
For another day of life and the present he was sent
She asks where he comes from and how his life has been spent
The same place as you he replies
She tells him that when he moves he glides
He tells her that he loves to look into her eyes

When she is gone he is again in his aloneness
And realizes life is so much better in togetherness
The lion and the wolf await the return
Of the she-wolf and the golden-haired lioness

Through the Dark

In the darkness of the night I find you
Through the moonless sky you see me
Through your clothes, through your skin, I feel you
Through your mouth through your tongue you touch me
Through the ebbs and through the flows
There appears something here that we both know
Time passes there is space
And then again I see your face
As I feel you you make me feel
And then it continues to make us reel
Seasons change and again it's fall
A year gone by and through it all
A time to reap a time to sow
There appears something here that we both know

To a Rolling Stone

Street Fightin' Man with nine lives
You got soul and you survive
You're the man that we all know
You're the king of rock 'n' roll
You Got the Silver and you got the gold
So let's have a drink to a Rolling Stone

A telecaster and a three thirty-five
A couple of chords with a whole lot of drive
It's Only Rock 'n' Roll, but it keeps you alive
So let's raise a glass to a Rolling Stone

Time Waits For No One, but *Time Is On My Side*
We've spent some time together, it's been one hell of a ride
So just *Paint it Black*
Mister Jumpin' Jack

Main offender the human riff
Monkey Man I get your drift
Captain Tongue, you stand alone
Satisfaction is guaranteed
Maybe *The Last Time*
So just *Let It Bleed*
He gathers no moss
He stands alone
So let's raise a glass to a Rolling Stone
Let's have a drink to a Rolling Stone

Tradition

A beautiful Friday evening at sunset
Ancient stones burning aglow
Reflecting the sun setting low
As it has done
For millennia centuries and years
Through far too many tears
This is my tradition

Spring sky azure blue
Domes alight of blazing gold
A sacred place
From days of old
Singing birds dancing in electrified air
Through alleys plazas and stairs
Where countless millions have walked before me
This is my tradition
Placing my hands onto thousands years old stones
I am transfixed
As if gazing into an infinity mirror
Where all of my ancestors throughout time
Are right here and right now looking back at me
Present in the timeless eternity
I have fulfilled their collective destiny
This is my tradition
I can softly hear them whispering
"NEXT YEAR IN JERUSALEM"
And I said to all of them
I have fulfilled your mission
Here I am now for all of you
Thank you for passing on my tradition

Standing at walls where so many secrets are hidden
Where holy men extend their arms in benediction
A sacred place where prayers and blessings are given
Ancient stones of timeless inspiration
From generation to generation
This is my tradition
This is my JERUSALEM

Radiator Man

You wear tight jeans
And you like a man with means
You wear high heels
and you drive hot wheels
I'm your radiator man
I'm gonna heat you hot as I can
I'm your radiator man
Your world's biggest fan

You got me hot wired
Got me on fire
You make my blood boil
I'm gonna spring like a coil
I'm your radiator man
Gonna kiss you hot as I can
I'm your radiator man
Gonna love you best I can

You're the lady of cool
Nobody's fool
A real hot mama
And the queen of drama
I'm your radiator man
Hotter than a frying pan
I'm your radiator man
Gonna hold you tight as I can

Un Poeme Pour Murielle

Murielle *ma belle*
Tu es mon coeur
            Tu es mon fleur
                  Ma Murielle

Murielle mon amour
            Je suis tres heureux
                  Je t'aime beaucoup
                        Ma Murielle

Murielle mon cher
            Ce sont les mots que je veux te dire
                  Tu es mon ame
                        Ma Murielle

Murielle tu fais briller mes yeux
            Je veux entre dans la vie avec toi
                  Tu es l' parfum de Dieu
                        Ma Murielle

Murielle tu fais voler mon esprit
            C'est ce que je veux dire
                  Ce que je veux tu saches
                        Je t'adore ma Murielle

Until

I have been to Monaco and Acapulco
       Amalfi and Capri too
But I have never been anywhere
       Until I just met you

I have journeyed to Paris, Milan,
       Tuscany Rome and Corfu
Seen the David the Mona Lisa
       Musee Picasso and Dali too
But I have never seen anything
       Until I just saw you

I have climbed mountain tops
       And hills of morning dew
And I have swum the Atlantic, the Pacific
       And the Mediterranean too
But I have never swum anywhere
       Until I swam to you

I have lived in forests and deserts
       On seaside cliffs so blue
In cities countries and jungles
       So many places I have been it's true
But I have never been anywhere
       Until I have been with you

I could be anywhere at any time or any place
        Just so I could be close enough
                To gaze upon your face
I would be under the darkest cloud
        Or under sunny skies
                Just to be close enough
                        To look into your eyes

Waterfall

May we stand by your flowing waters
　　May we sit by your cool
　　　　In your sound
　　Contained in your life stream
　　　　We drink from your source
　　　　　　Nourished we thrive
　　　　　Awake and alive
　　　　　　　We are in you
Waterfall

Not afraid am I of being swept away
　　By the rush of your force
Though your currents may at time be rough
　　I know you will lead me to still waters
　　　I know that in your kiss
　　　　We flow into the ocean of bliss

Waterfall
　　May we stand
　　　　By your flowing waters

When a Tree Falls

When a tree falls
Laying in transformation
Once tall and vibrant in life
Now still in regeneration

When a tree falls
Creating new rotation
Life into death death into life
A continuous illusion

When a tree falls
Can you hear the sound
The circle of life
Turning around and around

Wherever

Wherever I may travel
Wherever I may roam
Wherever I may wander
I am always in my home

Whether on the mountain or by the ocean's side
Under the full moon or gazing at sunrise
As long as you are with me
I am always in my home

Familiar I may be through locations that range
Like the weather seasons and years
And the friends and lovers that change
As long as you are with me
I am always in my home

When I am in need of new direction
Or should arise a course correction
I can always trust my decisions are right
As long as you are with me
I know I can follow the light
As long as you are with me
I am always in my home

Love Zone

A day in the city full of people
Or a night in the country all alone
It doesn't matter where we are sweetheart
We are in the love zone

Are you my muse my inspiration
A poem of words put on paper
Are you a goddess vision my meditation
Or are you the answer to my prayer

How did this happen
At this time of our lives
Did we miss each other before
What are we to realize

Are we past lovers once lost
Floating on life's oceans wave tossed
Brought together at this time and place
Feels so familiar warm and safe

The seeds of life have been sown
We are in the love zone

Who Are You?

Who are you
that you come to me so completely
Who am I
that I am open to you so freely
How did we know that this would be
that you always were inside of me
Did we have to travel through time and space
just to remember that we come from the same place
So familiar it seems
As if we are in a dream
And knowing you
Have made our dreams come true

Silver and Gold

I found a piece of silver
with a precious stone of green
How does it feel
to be truly seen

I found a piece of gold
with a priceless stone of blue
How does it feel
now that I found you

I found two little streams
flowing into the same river
A heart and a soul
looking into the mirror

A little piece of silver
with a heart in its center
And a little piece of gold
with a soul in which to enter

How lucky am I
to find such treasure
To know happiness joy
peace and pleasure

How blessed am I
To flow in the life force
And bask in your light
Directly from the source

Wild Wolf

In the forest in the dark
Roams a beast with a pounding heart
In the wild deep in the wood
Is it malevolent or misunderstood
Right or wrong is a human sense
So we look for reasons
The wolf is instinctive
Natural like the seasons
And through dreams from the lair
The scent travels through the air
With raging feelings pent
Roams the wild wolf

Sole Survivor

There is a disruption in the field
Something is not the same
There is a crack in the ground
A blow in my mind
A tear in my soul
A rip in my gut
A bleed in my heart
I am shocked and stunned
Something has drastically changed
I am confused
Reality has been bent out of shape
and will never be the same
She is gone
They are all gone
Only the fading wake of the memories
Of what once was a life a love a family
And I alone am the sole survivor
The final repository of all that once was
The joys and the pains
The love and all it's stains
The first born and the last
to cherish and keep all of what used to be

Prayer

Now I lay me down to sleep
I pray to God my soul to keep
I put my head on the bed
And hope I don't wake up dead

I sat with Buddha to meditate
And practiced yoga to levitate
I saw Jesus in my dream
He told me of the love supreme

I danced to Hare Krishna Hare Rama
And chanted Jai Guru Deva
I wear a tallit and recite the Shema
And sing hallelujah hallelujah

When the time arrives for the great ascent
I'll be ready for the final event
Enlightened beings have shown the way
To the stairway to heaven do I pray

About the Author

Samuel Gluck was born August 18, 1947, to an eastern European immigrant family and raised in The Bronx and Yonkers, New York. He attended the University of Bridgeport and graduated with a bachelor of arts degree in history in 1970.

Sam had a 45-year career in financial services. He was an adjunct professor at Pace University in New York, where he taught yoga and meditation for 45 years. He also taught classes, courses, and workshops throughout the New York area.

His first poem, included herein, is Island Lady, which he wrote in 1970 and which was published in 1994 in "A Far Off Place" by the National Library of Poetry. Since then his poems have been published in various anthologies.

His inspiration and muse is nature, which is his home, love, which has been his blessing, and God, the source of his being.

Visit samuelgluckpoet.com for more.

About Orenaug Mountain Publishing (OMP)

It is the vision of Orenaug Mountain Publishing (www.orenaugmountainpublishing.com) to be a beacon for poetic expression and to create a platform for poets to share their work with the world.

We seek to champion the art of poetry of writers around the world by publishing high-quality work that challenges, inspires, and connects readers to the human experience.

We do this through several themed anthology projects a year and via the online Orenaug Mountain Poetry Journal at www.orenaugmountainpoetry.net.

Visit our website to learn more about what we do, and to find out how to take part in our anthologies or our poetry journal.

www.ingramcontent.com/pod-product-compliance
Lightning Source LLC
Chambersburg PA
CBHW080520090426
42734CB00015B/3118